Charles Myrick Thurston

Descendants of John Pitman

The First of the Name in the Colony of Rhode Island

Charles Myrick Thurston

Descendants of John Pitman
The First of the Name in the Colony of Rhode Island

ISBN/EAN: 9783337380007

Printed in Europe, USA, Canada, Australia, Japan

Cover: Foto ©ninafisch / pixelio.de

More available books at **www.hansebooks.com**

OF

JOHN PITMAN,

THE FIRST OF THE NAME

IN THE

COLONY OF RHODE ISLAND.

COLLECTED BY

CHARLES MYRICK THURSTON.

STEMMATA QUID FACIUNT?

NEW YORK:

THE TROW & SMITH BOOK MANUFACTURING CO., 46, 48, 50 GREENE ST

1868.

Copies of this pamphlet will be sent to those who have furnished information. Other copies will be sent, post-paid, to those interested, who are willing to contribute toward the cost of printing.

Owing to the destruction of the early records of the town of Newport, it has been impossible to obtain a full account of the descendants of JOHN PITMAN.

The undersigned has collected, from public and private records, the contents of this pamphlet, which it is believed will be interesting to the descendants now living, and enable them to trace their families back to the first settler of the name in Rhode Island.

It is hoped that hereafter some one may continue the work.

CHARLES MYRICK THURSTON.

NEW ROCHELLE, Westchester Co., N. Y., 1868.

THE NAME IN ENGLAND.

The name PITMAN is said to be derived from residence in vicinity of a pit.

JOHANNES PITEMAN is mentioned in Hundred Rolls, 1273.

A family of PITMAN has been seated at Dunchideock-house, County Devon, for several generations, and is recorded in the parish registers from the year 1552.

ARMS.

Quarterly, ar. and or., an eagle displ. with two heads gu. Crest: A martlet upon a shell.

PITMAN, Woodbridge, Co. Suffolk, Gu. two poleaxes in saltier, or., headed ar., betw. four mullets of the last. Crest: A moor's arm ppr. escarroned of his colors, advancing a poleaxe, the handle or., headed ar.

PITMAN, same arms. Crest: A rock sa.

GEOFFREY PITMAN was sheriff of Suffolk Co. in 1625.
PITMAN, in Yorkshire pedigrees.

THE NAME IN ENGLAND.

The name PITMAN is said to be derived from residence in vicinity of a pit.

JOHANNES PITEMAN is mentioned in Hundred Rolls, 1273.

A family of PITMAN has been seated at Dunchideock-house, County Devon, for several generations, and is recorded in the parish registers from the year 1552.

ARMS.

Quarterly, ar. and or., an eagle displ. with two heads gu. Crest: A martlet upon a shell.

PITMAN, Woodbridge, Co. Suffolk, Gu. two poleaxes in saltier, or., headed ar., betw. four mullets of the last. Crest: A moor's arm ppr. escarroned of his colors, advancing a poleaxe, the handle or., headed ar.

PITMAN, same arms. Crest: A rock sa.

GEOFFREY PITMAN was sheriff of Suffolk Co. in 1625.
PITMAN, in Yorkshire pedigrees.

THE NAME IN NEW ENGLAND.

Thomas Pitman, born 1614, settled at Marblehead, Mass.
Mark Pitman, born 1622, settled at Marblehead, Mass.
William Pitman, born 1662, settled at Oyster River, N. H.
Nathaniel Pitman, settled at Salem, Mass., in 1630.
Joseph Pitman, settled at Charlestown, Mass., in 1658.
Jonathan Pitman, settled at Stratford, Conn., in 1681.

A resemblance has been seen in several instances between some of the descendants of JOHN PITMAN, and those of the other families of Pitman in New England. It is possible that HENRY PITMAN, the father of John, may have been a relative of some of the above-named early New England settlers, as New Providence was settled in 1666, by emigrants from England, and from the other colonies in America.

The Bahamas were discovered by Columbus in 1492; first settled by the English in 1629; expelled by the Spaniards in 1641; recolonized by the English in 1666; expelled by the French and Spaniards in 1703. When New Providence was uninhabited, or nearly so, about two hundred heads of white families were settled in Eleuthera and Harbor islands. The islands were formally ceded to the English in 1783.

1 HENRY PITMAN was one of the first settlers of Nassau, New Providence, one of the Bahama islands (probably about 1666).

His grand-daughter, MARY DAVENPORT, in her deposition, made February 7, 1763, testified that her grandfather was "one of the first settlers, built a house, planted fruit trees, and made great improvements." "He dwelt there about fifteen years, more or less, and died about the time of fishing for the Plate wreck,* and that his house was burned in the depredations of enemies; all of which she has been told by her parents, who showed her the ruins of her said grandfather's house."

Children :

2   I. JOHN, born 1663; died 1711.

2 JOHN PITMAN (Henry), married MARY SAUNDERS. He lived first at Harbor Island, thence he removed to Nassau, New Providence, and settled on and took possession of the tract of land, plantations, and improvements, made by his father. On the 26th January, 1699, he received from

* Plate wreck. Sir William Phipps made an expedition in search of treasure wrecked in a Spanish vessel. He found a wreck at the Bahamas, but the value recovered from it proved insufficient to defray the expense of the voyage. He returned to London in 1684. Afterward he found the treasure near Port de la Plata, Hispaniola, and returned to England in 1687.

Gov. Webb a grant and confirmation of said land.* He built a house near the ruins of that of his father, cultivated and made improvements, erected a ship-yard, and built several vessels; and lived there until the taking and burning of New Providence by the French and Spaniards in July, 1703. His house having been burned, he removed first to Currant Island, thence to Thesa Island, and finally, in 1710, to the colony of Rhode Island, and settled in Newport.

He died Nov. 21, 1711, aged 48 years.—His widow, Mary, died December 1, 1711, aged 45 years.

Children :

3   I. John, born at Harbor Island; died single.

4   II. Mary, born 1693, at Harbor Island; married Ebenezer Davenport, Feb. 12, 1714.

NASSAU, New Providence.

* John, Earl of Bath, Palatine, the Lord Craven, the Lord Berkeley, Anthony Ashley, George, Lord Carteret, and Sir John Colleton, Baronet, the true and absolute Lords and proprietors of New Providence and the rest of the Bahama Islands, do hereby grant unto JOHN PITMAN a parcel of land to the eastward of the city, containing one hundred and fifty acres, English measure, butting and bounding westerly on the plantation known by Debit's Point; easterly on Susannah Woodfield's plantation; north to the sea; and south on land not taken up. To have and to hold to him, the said JOHN PITMAN, his heirs and assigns, forever, he and they yielding and paying to the said Lords proprietors, their heirs and assigns, a yearly rent of one penny per acre. Provided, further, that the said JOHN PITMAN doth plant and settle the said land within twelve months after date hereof, according as the law has provided in such cases. On default of which, the said land shall return to the Lords proprietors, and be free for the first adventurer. Given under our hand and public seal of this Government, in behalf of the said Lords proprietors, this twenty-sixth day of January, 1698–9.

         NICHOLAS WEBB, Governor,

         BARTHOLOMEW MESELER, for Lord Ashley,

         JOHN LEIGHTON, for Lord Carteret.

Passed the Secretary's office,

     EDWARD VAUGHAN, Secretary.

Registered in Newport, R. I., July 29, 1720.

         WILLIAM CODDINGTON, Town Clerk.

5   III. JOSEPH, born March 16,
         1695, at Harbor Island.
         See Nos. 11 to 18.

6   IV. BENJAMIN, born 1697,   Samuel Whaitman
         at New Providence.   appointed guardian
         See Nos. 19 to 118.   January 7, 1712.

7   V. JAMES, born 1700, at New
         Providence. See Nos.
         119 to 126.

8   VI. SAMUEL, born 1701, at
         New Providence. See
         Nos. 127 to 269.   Arnold Collins ap-

9   VII. MOSES, born 1702, at   pointed guardian,
         Thesa Island. See Nos.   January 7, 1712.
         270 to 274.

10   VIII. ——, born in Newport, R. I.

This estate in Nassau was never alienated by the family.
After the death, in 1711, of John Pitman, his son, Joseph Pitman,
gave a lease of the premises to his uncle, Saunders. After the
death of Benjamin Pitman, in 1762, the family united in collect-
ing evidence of their claim to the property, and concluded to send
John Pitman, Esq. (the son of Joseph), to New Providence, to
recover possession thereof. But it appearing that this John Pitman intended to claim the property for himself, by virtue of the
English law of primogeniture, the other members of the family
would not consent, and before any definite arrangement could be
made, the war of the Revolution commenced, and the estate was
lost by the British statute of limitations. A search has been
made in Nassau for farther particulars. Their records only go
back to 1723, and the name of Pitman does not appear thereon.
In a letter, dated New Providence, August 10, 1762, to her
dear cousin, Benjamin Pitman, Sen., at Newport, R. I., Martha
Light, the daughter of —— and Jane Saunders, requests a
new lease, and states that her brother claims the land.

DESCENDANTS OF JOSEPH PITMAN, THE SECOND SON OF JOHN AND MARY.

5   JOSEPH PITMAN, of Newport (John², Henry¹). Married MARY WHAITMAN, Dec. 19, 1717. He died March 21, 1731, aged 36 years.

Children:

11   I. JOHN, born March 29, 1719. See Nos. 17 and 18.
12   II. Mary, born Jan. 1, 1721.
13   III. Samuel, born Jan. 15, 1723.
14   IV. Martha, born Oct. 9, 1725; married James Murphy, June 29, 1746.
15   V. Joseph, born May 19, 1729.
16   VI. Sarah, born Nov. 14, 1731; married William Bentley, Nov. 18, 1756.

---

11 JOHN PITMAN, of Newport (Joseph³, John², Henry¹). Married MARY SIMMONS. He died March 2, 1800, aged 81 years. His wife, Mary, died May 25, 1789, aged 73 years.

Children:

17   I. Elizabeth, died single, Feb. 8, 1801, aged 57 years.
18   II. Mary, died single, Dec. 12, 1833, aged 86 years; will proved 1834.

DESCENDANTS OF BENJAMIN PITMAN, THE THIRD SON OF JOHN AND MARY.

———◆———

6 BENJAMIN PITMAN, of Newport (John, Henry). Married Mary ————. He was a freeman May 5, 1741. He died Sept. 12, 1762, aged 65 years. His wife, Mary, died Nov. 19, 1746, aged 49 years.

Children:

19   I. Benjamin, died August 15, 1722, aged 16 months.
20   II. JOHN. See Nos. 25 to 106.
21   III. JAMES. See Nos. 107 to 118.
22   IV. Benjamin, died April 26, 1813, aged 84 years. His wife, Abigail, died March 19, 1796, aged 67 years.
23   V. Gilbert, baptized July 23, 1732; died August 23, 1769, aged 37 years.
24   VI. Mary, baptized Aug. 21, 1737; married Thomas Brown, Nov. 19. 1761.

————

20 JOHN PITMAN, of Newport (Benjamin, John, Henry). Married ABIGAIL, daughter of Andrew and Abigail (Plaisted) Nichols, May 6, 1750. He died December 27, 1768. His will was dated December 26, 1768, and proved February 6, 1769. His widow, Abigail, was admitted into Dr. Stiles' church, November 10, 1771, and her four children were baptized at the same time. In July, 1775, she removed to South Kingstown, where she died, June 17, 1780, aged 54 years.

Children :

25   I. Elizabeth, born 1753; married Thomas Courtane,
          Dec. 9, 1770; died Oct. 10, 1771, aged 18
          years.
26   II. JOHN, born June 27, 1757. See Nos. 31 to 60.
27   III. Mary, born June 10, 1758; died single, Sept. 21,
          1841.
28   IV. Andrew, born 1762; died Sept. 1766, aged 4 years.
29   V. THOMAS GILBERT, born May 8, 1764. See Nos.
          61 to 90.
30   VI. BENJAMIN, born Sept. 16, 1766. See Nos. 91
          to 106.

---

26 JOHN PITMAN, of Newport (John, Benjamin, John,
       Henry). Married NANCY BENNETT. He died May
       25, 1809, aged 52 years. His will was dated Nov. 29, 1808,
       and proved June 5, 1809. His widow died Sept. 16, 1828,
       aged 72 years.
Children :
31   I. John, born Sept. 2, 1786; married Hannah Mum-
          ford, Nov. 13, 1810; died Jan. 24, 1863.
32   II. GEORGE B., born July 5, 1788. See Nos. 41 to 45.
33   III. CHARLES, born March 3, 1790. See Nos. 46
          to 60.
34   IV. James, born August 3, 1791; married Elizabeth
          D. Wheeler, October 30, 1825.
35   V. Nancy, born January 9, 1793; died June 4, 1794.
36   VI. Sarah, born May 25, 1794; died October 18, 1795.
37   VII. Maria, born May 10, 1796; died August 27, 1796.
38   VIII. Elizabeth Ann, born January 6, 1798; married
          William H. Taylor, June 18, 1821.
          Children :
              1. Mary Anne, born 1822.
              2. Emily Antoinette, born 1824.
              3. James, born 1825.
              4. William Henry, born 1827.

5. Jane Eliza, born 1830.
6. John Pitman, born 1832.
7. George Alfred, born 1834.
8. Harriet Cushing, born 1836.
9. Amelia Frances, born 1841.

39   IX. William, born September 13, 1799; died October 4, 1799.

40   X. Henry, born September 6, 1800.

---

32 GEORGE B. PITMAN, of Pelham, Mass. (John, John, Benjamin, John, Henry). Married MARGARET D. GINNODA, January 27, 1814. He died April 28, 1861, aged 73 years.

Children:

41   I. Sarah, born Dec. 19, 1815; died Nov. 6, 1817.

Mrs. M. D. Pitman died April 29, 1817.

Second wife, ABIGAIL NICHOLS; married March 5, 1820; died March 27, 1845.

42   II. Phebe Ann, born March 27, 1821; married H. A. Bartlett, April 10, 1850.

43   III. Abigail, born Nov. 22, 1823; married L. H. Moulton, June 17, 1853.

Children:
1. Abby Eleanor, born 1854.
2. George Pitman, born 1856.
3. Martha Ann, born 1859.

44   IV. John Nichols, born May 19, 1828.

45   V. Sarah Elizabeth, born Dec. 3, 1834; married J. T. Moulton, July 11, 1857.

Child:
1. Ida Mary, born 1859.

---

33 CHARLES PITMAN, of Fall River (John, John, Benjamin,

John, Henry). Married AMY GORTON, March 31, 1811. He died July 26, 1855, aged 65 years.

Children:

46   I. John, born Feb. 26, 1812; died 1812.
47   II. Ann B., born July 4, 1813; died Sept. 14, 1843.
48   III. Julia E., born Jan. 18, 1816; married Francis Lincoln; died June 10, 1847.
49   IV. CHARLES E., born Nov. 8, 1818. See 54 to 56.
50   V. GEORGE W., born March 8, 1821. See 57 to 59.
51   VI. James M., born Sept. 23, 1823.
52   VII. Eliza T., born June 24, 1826; married George F. Baylis, April 12, 1854.
        Children:
            1. Ella Eudora, born 1855; died 1857.
            2. Frank M., born 1858.
53   VIII. JOHN H., born July 17, 1828. See No. 60.

_____

49 CHARLES E. PITMAN, of Somerset, Mass. (Charles, John, John, Benjamin, John, Henry). Married HARRIET E. POTTER, October 16, 1841.

Children:

54   I. Harriet, born Aug. 31, 1852.
55   II. Edward G., born Sept. 20, 1854.
56   III. William B., born Sept. 28, 1856.

_____

50 GEORGE W. PITMAN, of New Bedford (Charles, John, John, Benjamin, John, Henry). Married ELIZABETH PERKINS, April 1, 1850.

Children:

57   I. William Henry, born January 11, 1851.
58   II. George Nash, born Jan. 15, 1857.
59   III. Caroline Elizabeth, born March 1, 1865.

_____

53 JOHN H. PITMAN, of Fall River, Mass. (Charles, John, John, Benjamin, John, Henry). Married HANNAH J. TUCKER, October 22, 1855.

Child:

60   I. Mary O., born Feb. 12, 1861.

29 THOMAS G. PITMAN, of Newport (John, Benjamin, John, Henry). Married ABIGAIL, daughter of George and Elizabeth (Peckham) Hall, grand-daughter of Benjamin and Abigail (Babcock) Hall, g.-grand-daughter of William and Mary (Brownell) Hall, g.-g.-grand-daughter of Benjamin and Frances (Parker) Hall, and g.-g.-g.-grand-daughter of William and Mary Hall,* May 4, 1788. He was a Chief Justice of the Court of Common Pleas; an Elector in 1816 to elect James Madison President; was elected Treasurer of the State in 1815, and for fifteen successive years after. He died March 17, 1842, aged 78 years. His will was dated January 22, 1842, and proved April 21.

NOTE.—Frances Parker was the daughter of George and Frances Parker. Mary Brownell was the daughter of George and Susannah (Pearce) Brownell, and grand-daughter of Thomas and Ann Brownell. Susannah Pearce was the daughter of Richard and Susannah (Wright) Pearce. Susannah Wright was the daughter of George Wright. Abigail Babcock was the daughter of George and Elizabeth (Hall) Babcock, grand-daughter of John and Mary Babcock, and g.-grand-daughter of James and Sarah Babcock. Elizabeth Peckham was the daughter of Peleg and Elizabeth (Coggeshall) Peckham, grand-daughter of Joseph and Waite (Gould) Peckham, g.-grand-daughter of John and Sarah Peckham, and g.-g.-grand-daughter of John and Mary (Clarke) Peckham. Waite Gould was the daughter of Daniel and Waite (Coggeshall) Gould, and grand-daughter of Jeremy and Priscilla (Grovier) Gould. Waite Coggeshall was the daughter of John and Mary Coggeshall. Elizabeth Coggeshall was the daughter of Thomas and Mercy (Freeborn) Coggeshall, grand-daughter of Joshua and Sarah Coggeshall, g.-grand-daughter of Joshua and Joan (West) Coggeshall, and g.-g.-grand-daughter of John and Mary Coggeshall. Mercy Freeborn was the daughter of Gideon and Mary (Boomer) Freeborn, and grand-daughter of William and Mary Freeborn. Mary Boomer was the daughter of Matthew Boomer.

1842. His widow, Abigail, died April 1, 1842, aged 71 years.

Children:

61   I. BENJAMIN HENRY, born Nov. 28, 1789. See 69 to 84.

62   II. Abigail, born Aug. 5, 1791; died Aug. 10, 1791.

63   III. Eliza, born July 28, 1792; married William S. Nichols, March 26, 1815.

Children:
1. Thomas P., born 1816; married Lydia M. Foster.
2. Walter, born 1818; married Abby A. Mumford.
3. Rachel S., born 1822; married Simon Newton, Jr.
4. Abby P., born 1826; married W. B. Bliss.
5. Matilda B., born 1832.

64   IV. Thomas, born July 1, 1794; died Sept. 23, 1795.

65   V. Abigail, born April 21, 1796; married Rev. Ebenezer Colman, Jan. 17, 1819.

Children:
1. Abby P., born 1819; married Dr. W.R. Converse, Princeton, Ill.
2. Susan, born 1820; died 1825.
3. Emily, born 1823; married H. E. Baker, Detroit, Mich.
4. Elizabeth, born 1824; died 1825.
5. Susan, born 1826; died 1827.
6. Ebenezer, born 1831; married Jane E. Maltmon, Toronto, C. W.
7. George W., born 1834.

Rev. E. Colman died in Detroit, Mich., June 15, 1859.

66   VI. Rachel Hall, born July 9, 1799; married Charles M. Thurston, Sept. 6, 1818.

Children:
1. Charles Myrick, born 1819; married Caroline Marsh, 1843.

    2. Abby Pitman, born 1821; married
      Richard Lathers, 1846.
    3. Rachel Hall, born 1824; married
      Charles C. Barrington, 1843.
    4. Sophia Eliza, born 1827; married
      Allan Melville, 1847.
    5. Alfred Henry, born 1832; married
      Eliza S. Blunt, 1856; Mary S.
      Bankhead, 1864.
   Charles M. Thurston died in New York, May 6,
    1844.

67   VII. THOMAS GILBERT, born April 23, 1805. See
      Nos. 85 to 90.

68   VIII. Emily, born March 13, 1807; married Simon
      Newton, Jr., July 1, 1827; died Nov. 15, 1841.
      Child:
         1. Thomas Pitman, born 1838; mar-
           ried Louisa Knowles.

---

61 Rev. BENJAMIN H. PITMAN, of Newport (Thomas, John,
    Benjamin, John, Henry). Married MARY STANHOPE,
    Dec. 16, 1810. He died March 8, 1868, aged 78 years.
  Children:
69   I. Ann, born in Newport, Dec. 15, 1812; married Dr.
      Henry R. Vaille, Springfield, Mass., June 25,
      1838.
      Children:
         1. Edward Stanhope, born 1839; died
           1840.
         2. Henry Robert, born 1845.
         3. Thomas Pitman, born 1848.
      Mrs. Ann Vaille died Feb. 21, 1849.
70   II. Sarah Dunnell, born in Newport, March 31, 1815;
      married David Smith, Northampton, N. Y.,
      Oct. 28, 1838.
      Children:
         1. Henry, born 1840; died 1844.

Second husband, Jabez Gibbs, of Northampton,
N. Y. Married July 18, 1843.

  ·2. Edward Stanhope; died in Louisi-
   . ana, on Banks' expedition, 1863.

Third husband, William Ilsley, Harlem, N. Y.
Married February 1, 1860.

71   III. ROBERT HALL, born in Newport, June 10, 1817.
See Nos. 76 to 70.

72   IV. Mary Jane, born in Tiverton, May 3, 1819; married Dr. Ingersoll Leonard, Dec. 24, 1841.
     Children :
        1. Harriet Eliza, born 1844; died 1863.
        2. Mary Stanhope, born 1847; died
           1847.
        3. Augustine, born 1849.
        4. Jane, born 1851; died 1852.

73   V. Elizabeth Nichols, born in Goffestown, N. H., Aug.
17, 1821; married James Erwin, of Guilderland,
Sept. 26, 1846.
     Children :
        1. Henrietta, born 1848.
        2. Ann Pitman, born 1856.
        3. Elizabeth, born 1857.
        4. Benjamin James, born 1861; died
           1865.

74   VI. Abigail, born in Goffestown, N. H., Aug. 2, 1823;
married William S. Gibbs.
     Children :
        1. Mary Evelina, born 1855; died
           1855.
        2. Ella La Vere, born 1857.
William S. Gibbs died in Northampton, Sept. 7,
1861.

75   VII. THOMAS GILBERT, born in Goffestown, N. H.,
Sept. 30, 1825. See Nos. 81 to 84.

---

71 ROBERT H. PITMAN, of Albany (Benjamin, Thomas,

John, Benjamin, John, Henry). Married FREEDOM H. CLARK, in Brattleboro, Vt., October 17, 1839.

Children:

76   I. FRANK CLARK, born May 31, 1841. See No. 80.

Mrs. F. H. Pitman died Dec. 15, 1842.

Second wife, SOPHIA WOODCOCK. Married June 18, 1845.

77   II. Sophia Woodcock, born May 5, 1846.
78   III. Benjamin Henry, born July 19, 1848.
79   IV. Frederick Nathan, born Dec. 7, 1849.

---

76 FRANK C. PITMAN, of Albany (Robert, Benjamin, Thomas, John, Benjamin, John, Henry). Married MAR-GARET YATES, September 8, 1859.

Child:

80   1. Grace, born May 29, 1866.

---

75 THOMAS G. PITMAN, of New Haven (Benjamin, Thomas, John, Benjamin, John, Henry). Married HARRIET A. VANDUZEN, of New Hartford, Litchfield Co., Conn.

Children :

81   I. Edward Stanhope, born April 18, 1853.
82   II. Mary Stanhope, born Dec. 21, 1860; died Jan. 18, 1861.
83   III. Thomas Gilbert, born May 22, 1863.
84   IV. Ella Louisa, born Oct. 21, 1865.

---

67 THOMAS G. PITMAN, of Newport (Thomas, John, Benjamin, John, Henry). Married SARAH, daughter of George S. Sweet. He died September 21, 1846, aged 41 years.

Children:

85 I. Abby, born June 17, 1831; married Augustus
  French, Jan. 3, 1853.
   Child:
    1. Rachel Pitman, born Oct. 19, 1853.
86 II. Emily, born April 23, 1833.
37 III. Rachel Hall, born Dec. 31, 1835; died Nov. 19,
  1853.
88 IV. John, born July 8, 1837; married Mary S. Spring-
  er, Feb. 12, 1867.
89 V. Andrew, born Dec. 2, 1839.
90 VI. George, born Feb. 14, 1842.

---

30 BENJAMIN PITMAN, of Newport (John, Benjamin, John.
Henry). Married REMEMBER, daughter of William and
Abigail Goddard, August 6, 1794. He died June 9, 1811,
aged 45 years. His widow died July 28, 1840, aged 71
years.

Children:

91 I. Thomas Freebody, born Feb. 16, 1797; died June
  16, 1858.
92 II. Ann Maria, born Aug. 16, 1798.
93 III. BENJAMIN, born March 19, 1800. See Nos. 99
  to 101.
94 IV. Eliza Ann, born Oct. 4, 1801; married Joseph
  Crocker, March 7, 1831.
   Children:
    1. William Robinson, born 1833.
    2. Mary Jane, born 1834; died 1835.
    3. Benjamin Pitman, born 1836; mar-
     ried Mary Hathaway, 1860.
    4. Elizabeth Matilda, born 1837.
   Joseph Crocker died Dec. 20, 1837. His widow
   died March 29, 1866.
95 V. Jane, born 1803; died 1803.

96   VI. WILLIAM ROBINSON, born Aug. 6, 1805. See
Nos. 102 to 106.

97   VII. Mary, born Jan. 29, 1806.

98   VIII. Jane, born Dec. 3, 1807; married Jacob Sillo-
way, Oct. 9, 1848.

---

93 BENJAMIN PITMAN, of New Bedford (Benjamin, John,
Benjamin, John, Henry). Married MARY ANN CAR-
TER, October 16, 1823.

Children:

99   I. ROBERT CARTER, born March 16, 1825. See
No. 101.

100   II. Mary E., born Feb. 12, 1836; married William
Shepherdson, Oct., 1861; died March 17, 1862.

Mrs. Mary A. Pitman died Dec. 15, 1841, aged 43 years.
Second wife, ELIZABETH HALL. Married April 18, 1844.

---

99 ROBERT C. PITMAN, of New Bedford (Benjamin, Benjamin, John, Benjamin, John, Henry). Married FRANCES
R. THOMAS, Aug. 15, 1855.

Child:

101   I. Robert K., born July 1, 1857.

---

96 WILLIAM R. PITMAN, of New Bedford (Benjamin, John,
Benjamin, John, Henry). Married ESTHER M., daughter
of John and Sabra Thurston, November 24, 1828.

Children:

102   I. Harriet Elizabeth, born Sept. 20, 1829; married Rev.
Carlos Banning, April 7, 1852.

Children:

1. Matilda Thurston, born 1854.

2. William Carlos, born 1860; died 1864.

3. Arthur Staples, born 1862; died 1865.

4. Edwin Thomas, born 1864.

5. Mary Elizabeth, born 1866.

103   II. WILLIAM GODDARD, born Oct. 15, 1834. See No. 106.

Mrs. E. M. Pitman died Nov. 7, 1834.

Second wife, Ann A. Topham. Married March 25, 1836.

104   III. Theophilus Topham; married M. J. Davis, Nov. 27, 1866.

105   IV. Benjamin, born 1844; died 1844.

---

103 WILLIAM G. PITMAN, of Newport (William, Benjamin, John, Benjamin, John, Henry). Married EUGENIA S. BEMIS, March 14, 1864.

Child:

106   I. Bertha Staples, born Aug. 6, 1865.

---

21 JAMES PITMAN, of New London (Benjamin, John, Henry). Married ABIGAIL GREENE, February 22, 1757.

Children:

107   I. Abigail, born June 14, 1758.

108   II. Ann, born May 26, 1759.

109   III. Elizabeth, born Jan. 9, 1761.

110   IV. Gilbert, born Feb. 5, 1763.

111   V. Lucy, born Jan. 17, 1765.

112   VI. Benjamin, born Sept. 16, 1768.

113   VII. James, born March 30, 1776; married Sarah Crocker, May, 1799.

114   VIII. SAMUEL, born March 1, 1778. See Nos. 115 to 118.

114 SAMUEL PITMAN, of New London (James, Benjamin, John, Henry). Married EUNICE HOLT, November 10, 1799.

Children:
115   I. Samuel Gilbert, born Sept. 20, 1800.
116   II. Eliza Holt, born June 1, 1803.
117   III. Abigail Greene, born Aug. 11, 1806.
118   IV. William, born Sept. 2, 1808.

DESCENDANTS OF JAMES PITMAN, FOURTH SON OF JOHN AND MARY.

---

7 JAMES PITMAN, of Newport (John,² Henry¹). Married SARAH SPOONER, June 23, 1735. He died November 20, 1769, aged 60 years. His will was dated September 24, 1762, and proved December 4, 1769. His wife, Sarah, died June 26, 1768, aged 55 years.

Children:

119   I. Sarah, baptized July 4, 1736; married James Fox, Aug. 6, 1761.
120   II. Rachel, baptized Jan. 22, 1738; married William Downing.
121   III. JAMES, baptized April 20, 1740. See No. 126.
122   IV. Susannah, baptized April 18, 1742; married Lemuel Martin, March 22, 1744.
123   V. Elizabeth, baptized April 29, 1744; died April 5, 1769.
124   VI. William, baptized Oct. 26, 1746; will proved 1784.
125   VII. Elijah, baptized March 5, 1748; died April 19, 1771.

---

121 JAMES PITMAN, of Newport (James,³ John,² Henry¹). Married MERCY ELDRED. His will was dated October 5, 1774, and proved February 2, 1784.

Child:

126   I. Thomas Eldred, died in Calcutta in 1821, aged 49 years.

7. Horatio G., born 1778; married
Mary B. Pierce.
8. Deborah, born 1783.

131   V. SAMUEL, baptized March 29, 1741. See Nos. 149
to 199.

132   VI. MOSES, baptized March 27, 1743. See Nos. 200
to 208.

133   VII. PELEG, baptized Aug. 16, 1747. See Nos. 209
to 269.

134   VIII. Bridget, baptized Dec. 18, 1748; married George
Clarke, Oct. 21, 1772.

Children:

1. John.
2. ———; married ——— Larned.
3. Ann; married Rev. Isaac B. Pierce.
4. Mary.
5. George.
6. Peleg.

---

128 JOSEPH PITMAN, of Newport (Samuel, John, Henry).
Married MARY SORDIE.

Children:

135   I. Samuel.
136   II. Cary.
137   III. John.
138   IV. Rebecca.

---

129 SAUNDERS PITMAN, of Providence (Samuel, John,
Henry). Married MARY KINNICUTT, June 29, 1760.
He was a freeman in May, 1760. He died August 15,
1804, aged 73 years.

Children:

139   I. Amy, born May 6, 1761; married William Potter.

140   II. Rebecca, born March 11, 1763; married James Greene, Nov. 17, 1782; died July 7, 1806.

Children:

1. William, born 1783; married Minerva Bowers; Nuna Bennett.
2. Mary Kinnicutt, born 1785; married William Anthony.
3. Amy, born 1788; married Resolved Slack.
4. Elizabeth, born 1791; married Stephen Harris.
5. James Cary,   } Twins, born
6. Ebenezer Slocum, } 1793; died '95.
7. Abigail Susanna, born 1795; married John Greene.
8. Joseph Warren, born 1798; married Abby Frances Shaw; Mary Augusta Greene; Eliza Warland.
9. Sarah Ann; born 1801; married Stephen Arnold.
10. James Cary, born 1803; married Mary Ann Westcott.

141   III. Abigail, born March 2, 1765; married Ebenezer Johnson, June 9, 1793; died May 28, 1814.

Children:

1. George William, born 1794; died 1821.
2. Edward Saunders, born 1795; married Emily Dodge.
3. Emily, born 1797; died 1798.
4. Elizabeth Emily, born 1799; died 1806.
5. Martha Livermore, born 1800; died 1806.
6. Ebenezer, born 1803; died 1806.
7. Mary Saunders, born 1805; married Constant B. Mosher; George E. Blake.

8. Ebenezer Rice, born 1807; died
1834.
9. Sarah Pitman, born 1809; married
Joseph A. Blake.

142   IV. Susannah, born Nov. 25, 1766; married Ebenezer
R. Frost; died Dec. 7, 1795.

143   V. Samuel, born Dec. 22, 1768; died single, Aug. 4,
1813.

Mrs. Mary Pitman died June 13, 1770, aged 31 years.
Second wife, Amy Kinnicutt. Married February 9, 1772;
died October 17, 1817, aged 77 years.

144   VI. Mary, born April 13, 1773; married Samuel Dorrance, March 13, 1803; died Nov. 1, 1839.

Children:

1. Samuel, born 1804; died 1828.
2. Mary, born 1805; died 1829.
3. Saunders Pitman, born 1807; died
1830.
4. William Tully, born 1809; married
Amy Richmond.
5. Sarah Pitman, born 1812; died
1830.

145   VII. Anna, born Feb., 1775; married Jonathan Tiffany,
May 18, 1800; died Jan. 28, 1857.

146   VIII. Sarah, born Jan. 21, 1777; died May 2, 1806.

147   IX. John Kinnicutt, born Feb. 20, 1779; died single,
June 12, 1819.

148   X. Bernice Hale, born Sept. 30, 1781; died Sept. 5,
1782.

---

131 SAMUEL PITMAN, of Newport (Samuel, John, Henry).
Married REBECCA PROUD, May 5, 1772. He was a
freeman in May, 1768, and died in August, 1800.

Children:

149   I. SAMUEL. See Nos. 155 to 157.

150   II. Peleg; died in Boston, December, 1822, aged 49 years.

151   III. CHARLES, born July 11, 1775. See Nos. 158 to 179.

152   IV. George; died in South America.

153   V. Avis; married Samuel Taylor, Nantucket; died 1836.

Children:

1. Rebecca, born 1811; married George Wing.
2. Eliza, born 1813; married Edward Orpin.
3. Samuel, born 1816; married Mary Williston.
4. William, born 1818; married Henrietta Crocker.
5. Sarah Ann, born 1821; married Calvert Handy.

154   VI. ROBERT, born Feb. 7, 1785. See Nos. 180 to 199.

---

149 SAMUEL PITMAN, of Nantucket (Samuel, Samuel, John, Henry). Married ELIZABETH HALL. He was lost at sea.

Child:

155   I. JOHN, born April 15, 1799. See Nos. 156 and 157.

---

155 JOHN PITMAN, of Nantucket (Samuel, Samuel, Samuel, John, Henry). Married PHEBE FOLGER in 1826.

Children:

156   I. Frederick M., born 1833; married Elizabeth B. Gibbs in 1863.
157   II. Timothy C., born 1846.

---

151 CHARLES PITMAN, of Nantucket (Samuel, Samuel, John, Henry). Married SUSANNA MOOERS. He died February 22, 1852, aged 77 years. His widow died December 10, 1852, aged 83 years.

Children:

158   I. WILLIAM, born Nov. 2, 1801. See Nos. 163 to 169.
159   II. SAMUEL, born Jan. 26, 1806. See Nos. 170 to 175.
160   III. CHARLES, born July 5, 1808. See Nos. 176 to 179.
161   IV. Mary Ann, born 1811; married Charles Starbuck, 1831.
        Children:
            1. Winifred, born 1836.
            2. George B., born 1840.
            3. Benjamin, born 1842.
            4. Charles E., born 1845.
            5. Marietta, born 1847.
            6. Ella F., born 1849.
162   V. Lydia L., born 1815; married Samuel Swain, March 15, 1835; died Dec. 10, 1852.
        Children:
            1. Emily, born 1836.
            2. Helen M., born 1838.
            3. Matthew C., born 1841; died 1843.

---

158 WILLIAM PITMAN, of Nantucket (Charles, Samuel, Samuel, John, Henry). Married EUNICE F. COFFIN, February 14, 1827. This family removed to Ohio.

Children:

163   . I. Dr. Benjamin F., born Feb. 25, 1828; married Emmeline Wilcox, 1851; Sarah Curtis, 1858.
164   II. William E., born Sept. 24, 1832; married Alice Seigman. Killed in Virginia in 1864.
165   III. Priscilla F., born March 7, 1834; died in infancy.
166   IV. Alexander C., born Dec. 6, 1835; married Susan A. Burleigh, Springfield, Mass., 1859.

167   V. Ariel C., born July 13, 1837; married Susanna
       Riddell, Dec. 25, 1863.
168   VI. Phebe C., born Nov. 22, 1838.
169   VII. Emma B., born Aug. 29, 1840; married Julius F.
       Brayton, Dansville, N. Y.

---

159 SAMUEL PITMAN, of Nantucket (Charles, Samuel, Samuel,
    John, Henry). Married DEBORAH BAKER, October
    3, 1827.
    Children:
170   I. William B., born Sept. 6, 1828; married M. L.
       Colesworthy, March 18, 1857; died Sept. 6,
       1858.
171   II. Susan M., born Feb. 27, 1830; died Aug. 11, 1858.
172   III. Eliza B., born Dec. 20, 1839.
173   IV. Mary F., born June 6, 1843; died Sept., 1843.
174   V. Henry Lee, born April 23, 1846.
175   VI. Eugene, born Jan. 26, 1849; died Dec. 12, 1849.

---

160 CHARLES PITMAN, of Nantucket (Charles, Samuel,
    Samuel, John, Henry). Married MARY G. SWAIN,
    September 30, 1830.
    Children:
176   I. Charles, born April 22, 1834; died Jan. 28, 1840.
177   II. Maria C., born 1839; died 1852.
178   III. Elizabeth A., born March 8, 1840; married Charles
       B. Coffin in 1859.
179   IV. Abby C., born Sept. 12, 1842.

---

154 ROBERT PITMAN, of Nantucket (Samuel, Samuel, John,
    Henry). Married ELIZABETH HALL PITMAN, the

widow of his brother Samuel. He died December 11,
1865, aged 80 years.

Children:

180   I. Elizabeth, born July 13, 1806; married Benjamin
            Lawrence, Dec. 9, 1824.

            Children:
                1. William H., born 1825; married
                    Elizabeth A. Chase.
                2. Eliza P., born 1827; married Alfred
                    G. Alley.
                3. Robert S., born 1828. Lost at sea.
                4. Lydia M., born 1832; died 1834.
                5. Benjamin B., born 1837.
                6. Lydia S., born 1843.
                7. Rebecca, born 1851.

181   II. GEORGE, born Oct. 10, 1807. See Nos. 187 and
            188.
182   III. Rebecca, born Oct. 22, 1809; married Charles
            Wyer.
            Children:
                1. Rebecca G., born 1835.
                2. Benjamin F., born 1837; married
                    Mary F. Paddock.
183   IV. ROBERT, born 1811. See Nos. 189 and 190.
184   V. SAMUEL, born 1813. See No. 191.
185   VI. JAMES, born 1816. See Nos. 192 to 196.
186   VII. CHARLES, born 1818. See Nos. 197 to 199.

----

181 GEORGE PITMAN, of Nantucket (Robert, Samuel, Samuel,
        John, Henry). Married CHARLOTTE MEADER.

    Children:
187   I. Elizabeth H., born 1833; married Charles B. Hath-
            away.
188   II. Mary Abby, born 1840; married Joseph A. Star-
            buck, 1859.

183 ROBERT PITMAN, of Nantucket (Robert, Samuel, Samuel, John, Henry). Married ELIZABETH BARNARD.

Children:

189   I. Albert B., born 1844.
190   II. Samuel P., born 1848.

---

184 SAMUEL PITMAN, of Nantucket (Robert, Samuel, Samuel, John, Henry). Married REBECCA SWAIN. He died in 1843. His widow married Charles Elkins.

Child:

191   I. Susan S., born 1843.

---

185 JAMES PITMAN, of Nantucket (Robert, Samuel, Samuel, John, Henry). Married AMELIA WORTH, August, 1841.

Children:

192   I. Mary E., born July, 1843; married George F. Coffin, 1860.
193   II. Charlotte A., born 1847.
194   III. James F., born 1850.
195   IV. Emma, born 1853.
196   V. Charles Henry, born 1855.

---

186 CHARLES PITMAN, of Nantucket (Robert, Samuel, Samuel, John, Henry). Married ELIZABETH F. SWAIN.

Children:

197   I. Elizabeth, born 1848.

Mrs. Elizabeth F. Pitman died in 1849.

Second wife, PHEBE F. SWAIN, who died in 1855.

198   II. Ann S.

3

199   III. Phebe.

---

132 MOSES PITMAN, of Newport (Samuel, John, Henry).
      Married PHEBE WEEDEN.
      Children:
200   I. ISAAC. See Nos. 204 to 208.
201   II. Abigail; married John Coit.
202   III. George; married Mary Spiers.
203   IV. Rebecca; married —— Hyer.

---

200 ISAAC PITMAN, of Newport (Moses, Samuel, John,
      Henry). Married LYDIA BARKER. His will was dated
      July 12, 1821, and proved June 2, 1828.
      Lydia Pitman's will was dated September 17, 1845, and
      proved April 4, 1859.
      Children:
204   I. William.
205   II. Henry S.
206   III. Phebe V.; married Luther Lyon.
207   IV. Mary Ann; married —— Chace.
208   V. Isaac A.

---

133 PELEG PITMAN, of Bristol (Samuel, John, Henry).
      Married MARY WARDWELL. He died in 1812, aged
      65 years.
      Children:
209   I. SAMUEL, born 1771. See Nos. 218 to 240.
210   II. BENJAMIN, born 1774. See Nos. 241 to 264.
211   III. Mary, born 1775; died single, 1792.
212   IV. WILLIAM, born 1776. See Nos. 265 and 266.
213   V. NATHANIEL, born 1778. See Nos. 267 to 269.

214   VI. Rebecca, born 1780; died single, 1836.
215   VII. John A., born 1784; died single, 1856.
216   VIII. Allen W., born 1788; died single, 1790.
217   IX. Peter M.

—— 1590387

209 SAMUEL PITMAN, of Bristol (Peleg, Samuel, John, Henry). Married —— INGRAHAM. He died in 1815, aged 41 years.

Children:

218   I. JAMES D., born 1795. See No. 227.
219   II. JOSIAH H., born 1800. See Nos. 228 to 233.
220   III. SAMUEL, born 1802. See Nos. 234 and 235.
221   IV. Sarah, born 1804; married David Waldron.
222   V. George, born 1806; died 1825.
223   VI. Abby, born 1808.
224   VII. Ann, born 1810; married Samuel S. Munro.

        Children:
        1. Anna, born 1844.
        2. Benjamin, born 1859.

225   VIII. JOHN H., ⎫ born 1814. See Nos. 236 to 240.
              ⎬ Twins
226   IX. Elizabeth, ⎭ born 1814; married Nathan B. Heath.

        Children:
        1. Nathan H., born 1846.
        2. Mary; married Lyman W. Dean.
        3. Arnold H., born 1852.
        4. Edwin L., born 1850.

218 JAMES D. PITMAN, of Bristol (Samuel, Peleg, Samuel, John, Henry). Married MARY INGRAHAM.

Child:

227   I. Mary Anna, born 1822; died Sept. 29, 1841.

219 JOSIAH H. PITMAN, of Bristol (Samuel, Peleg, Samuel,
John, Henry). Married HANNAH LINDSAY.
Children:
228   I. Susan P., born September, 1825.
229   II. Samuel, born June, 1827.
230   III. Sarah H., born December, 1829.
231   IV. Josiah, born September, 1831.
232   V. Josiah, born August, 1834.
233   VI. George, born December, 1837.

220 SAMUEL PITMAN, of Bristol (Samuel, Peleg, Samuel,
John, Henry). Married MARY JANE STEWART.
Children:
234   I. Mary Jane, born 1835.
235   II. Samuel S., born 1837.

225 JOHN H. PITMAN, of Bristol (Samuel, Peleg, Samuel,
John, Henry). Married ELIZA SLADE.
Children:
236   I. Harriet F., born February, 1841.
237   II. Elizabeth H., born September, 1842.
238   III. Mary Anna, born May, 1845.
239   IV. Wilbor F., born March, 1848; died May, 1855.
240   V. George H., born June, 1857; died July, 1857.

210 BENJAMIN PITMAN, of Bristol (Peleg, Samuel, John.
Henry). Married LUCY KENT. He died in 1848, aged
74 years.
Children:
241   I. Ruth, born 1802.

242   II. BENJAMIN, born 1804. See Nos. 246 to 256.
243   III. Mary W., born 1806; married Thomas Norris,
        Dec. 31, 1829.
        Children :
            1. Jeremiah.
            2. Rebecca A.
            3. Mary F.
244   IV. WILLIAM HENRY, born 1809. See Nos. 257
        to 260.
245   V. JOSIAH KENT, born 1811. See Nos. 261 to 264.

---

242 BENJAMIN PITMAN, Jr., of Bristol (Benjamin, Peleg,
    Samuel, John, Henry). Married ELIZABETH REY-
    NOLDS. He died in 1862, aged 58 years. This family
    removed to Lamont, Michigan.
    Children :
246   I. Caroline, born Oct. 9, 1831.
247   II. Mary, born Oct. 9, 1831; died April 15, 1846.
248   III. Benjamin, born Nov. 19, 1833; died April 3, 1840.
249   IV. Helen, born Sept. 18, 1837; died March 30, 1840.
250   V. Benjamin, born March 21, 1841; died Nov. 9, 1845.
251   VI. Elizabeth, born June 5, 1842.
252   VII. Charles, born Dec. 14, 1843.
253   VIII. Helen, born Aug. 28, 1845.
254   IX. Mary, born June 5, 1847.
255   X. Georgianna, born May 12, 1850.
256   XI. Josephine, born March 31, 1853.

---

244 WILLIAM H. PITMAN, of Bristol (Benjamin, Peleg,
    Samuel, John, Henry). Married MARY HAWES.
    Children :
257   I. William H., born September, 1840.
258   II. John H., born June, 1842; died November, 1844.

259   III. Francis, born February, 1844; died March, 1844.
260   IV. Andrew F., born November, 1845.

---

245 JOSIAH K. PITMAN, of Bristol (Benjamin, Peleg, Samuel,
       John, Henry). Married ELIZA MANCHESTER.
       Children:
261   I. Josiah.
262   II. George.
263   III. Sarah.
264   IV. Julia.

---

212 WILLIAM PITMAN, of Bristol (Peleg, Samuel, John,
       Henry). Married THURSEY MAXFIELD. He died in
       1810, aged 34 years.
       Children:
265   I. Allen, born 1804; died 1850.
266   II. William, born 1808; died 1840.

---

213 NATHANIEL PITMAN, of Bristol (Peleg, Samuel, John,
       Henry). Married ELIZABETH SMITH. He died in
       1814, aged 36 years.
       Children:
267   I. Ellen S., born 1808; married Jeremiah D. Liscomb;
           died 1836.
               Children:
                   1. Raymond, born 1832; died 1836.
                   2. Ellen P., born 1836; married
                       Charles Hosmer.
268   II. Hezekiah J., born 1811.
269   III. Charlotte C., born 1814; married Alfred Luther.

Children:

1. Anna, born 1838.
2. Ellen, born 1840.
3. Alfred E., born 1845.
4. Winfield S., born 1848.
5. Manton, born 1854.

DESCENDANTS OF MOSES PITMAN, SIXTH SON OF JOHN AND MARY.

———◆———

9 MOSES PITMAN, of Newport (John, Henry). Married MARTHA, daughter of Richard Clarke. He was a freeman May 2, 1738. He was chosen Deacon of the Second Congregational Church April 26, 1741. He died April 27, 1760, aged 58 years. His widow died December 22, 1766, aged 63 years.

Children :

270   I. Clarke, baptized 1729; died Dec. 23, 1730.

271   II. Reed, baptized 1730; died April 15, 1731.

272   III. Alice, ⎰ baptized July 30, 1732; died Sept. 21,
               ⎱ Twins.   [1745.

273   IV. Martha, ⎱ baptized July 30, 1732 ; married John Cary, July 30, 1755.

        Child :

            1. Alice ; named in the will of her grandmother.

274   V. Hannah, baptized Aug. 10, 1734 ; married William Bentley, March 12, 1771.

MARRIAGES AND DEATHS.

MARRIED.

275 Mary Pitman, Newport, to Thomas Davenport, July 22, 1732.
276 Elizabeth Pitman, Newport, to Alexander Swan, Nov. 24, 1742.
277 Frederick Cobb Pitman, Newport, to Lydia Strengthfield, Oct. 27, 1765.

DIED.

278 Peter Pitman, Providence, aged 36, Dec. 13, 1820.
279 Ann Pitman, Providence, aged 62 (widow of Isaac), Nov. 14, 1833.
280 William W. Pitman, Providence, aged 41, Dec. 27, 1838.
281 R. H. Pitman, Savannah, Oct. 8, 1839.

No information has been received of any descendants of the following persons:

Fourth Generation.

13 Samuel,
15 Joseph.

Fifth Generation.

110 Gilbert,
112 Benjamin,
113 James,
135 Samuel,
136 Cary,
137 John,
202 George,
217 Peter M.

Sixth Generation.

40 Henry,
115 Samuel G.,
118 William,
204 William,
205 Henry S.,
208 Isaac A.

INDEX TO PITMANS.

GENERAL INDEX.